Real is Better Than Perfect

Stories and sayings for self-healing

Real is Better Than Perfect

Stories and sayings for self-healing

DOROTHY BALDWIN SATTEN, PhD

With Leslie Carol Baer Dinkel

Designed by Betsey Binét

Limited Edition

HOPEDANCING PUBLISHING 2006

Xela AID Partnerships for Self Reliance/Local Hope
111 West Ocean Boulevard, 4th Floor, Long Beach, California 90802
Mailing Address: 65 Pine Avenue, #404, Long Beach, California 90802
info@xelaaid.org

FIRST EDITION
April 2006, in a limited edition of 5,000 hardbound copies, of which
1,000 were signed and numbered by the author.

SECOND EDITION
March 2013, in an addition of 15,000 paperback copies.

THIRD EDITION
January 2019, paperback and ebook

Library of Congress Cataloguing-in-Publication Data
• Satten, Dorothy Baldwin 1932-2013
• Baer Dinkel, Leslie Carol 1958-
"Real is Better than Perfect | Stories and sayings for self-healing"
Dorothy Baldwin Satten. 1st ed.
ISBN 1-4243-0041-X (cloth)
ISBN 13: 978-1-7328856-2-2 (paperback)
ISBN 13: 978-1-7328856-1-5 (ebook)
1. Inspiration 2. Self-help 3. Personal growth
4. Interpersonal relationships

This book is dedicated to the memory of my wise Italian mother, Carolina Leonida Posterero, who taught me so much about *abundanza!*—generosity of spirit. It is further dedicated to my children, my stepchildren, my grandchildren, and my students and clients who continue to teach me about love and courage. And to my husband Mort, who daily reminds me what love means, and what love asks.

Zerka Toeman Moreno, the co-creator and a master teacher of psychodrama, is a scholar, one of my most important mentors, and a lifelong friend. For her encouragement and support, I will be forever grateful.

To Leslie and Betsey, two dream weavers who spun my dream into a beautiful cloth of many colors!

DOROTHY BALDWIN SATTEN

CONTENTS

AUTHOR'S NOTE

*F*OR MANY, MANY YEARS, I have wanted to write a book. I wanted to write something especially insightful, something that would help people become their own therapists. As a therapist, I always believed it was my job to work myself out of a job, because after all, therapy is not life—life is life.

I suppose it has taken me decades to follow through because as a former teacher of history, I thought it would be presumptuous to write a book—everything valuable had already been written! I also told myself the story that I didn't have the time as my dear husband and partner in Westwood Institute, Mort Satten, and I traveled the world sharing what we've learned over three decades as psychodramatists. Psychodrama has been such a blessing in my life that, especially in recent years (and having had a stroke), I've felt an urgency to pass it on in person. And so a book, or books, have had to wait.

I agreed to focus a bit of time on this book of sayings and stories after much cajoling from my friends, family, and psychodrama students—and with some of my own words being used to put me in a double-bind, such as, "It doesn't matter where you start, just that you start." And of course, "Real is better than perfect," too, has been used to that end. And so now, after many years in the making, comes this first book.

Much of what you'll read herein is original and draws from my own journey of self-discovery, now in my seventy-fifth year. I am compelled to point out, also, that some of what you'll read has been borrowed and compiled throughout the years, like my father's wisdom, "Life is like thin ice. If you're walking on thin ice, you may as well dance!" In each case of borrowing I offer my deep appreciation for the wisdom shared with me, and on the following pages the source, where known, is happily credited.

Those of you who are not familiar with me or with psychodrama may ask, "Why this book?" I have learned that each of us in this world—no matter how wonderful and supportive our families and friends, no matter what ethnicity or religion we are, what our economic status or what country we hail from—have a wounded child within. This child may not have been wanted, or not listened to. She may have lost all hope of having her needs met; or he may have been unable to become his own person, leave home and find a happy life. The material contained in this book aims to point the way to healing that wounded child.

You'll find herein, also, that some sayings which are similar to one another appear in different sections of the book. These reflect the various ways I've related them over the years, allowing my truth to shift and grow. They appear here with the hope that each form will be useful in a slightly different way to each reader, as they have been to me over the years as I've grown.

What I share on these pages, I have regularly shared with participants in my psychodrama training groups with the intent of helping to awaken the therapist within them—the best therapist they could ever have. It is a collection of stories and sayings of realization that have helped me live my own life much more authentically, and so, with much more of myself available to experience my life.

I would be remiss at this point if I didn't explain a little about psychodrama. It is a powerful, action-method of therapy from which I gained the insights that led to this book. The practice of psychodrama creates a map through the terrain of your life. The method was developed by psychiatrist Jacob Levy Moreno in the 1920s, derived from his "Theatre of Spontaneity for Children," his seminal work in 1911. As a young medical student,

Moreno watched children at play in the parks of Vienna. He noticed that by taking on the roles of characters in their lives, the children seemed to be able to express feelings in a healing way. He put forth the idea that events are stored in the body's memory, and that by creating a context in which these memories can be evoked, people can revisit scenes in their lives—pleasant or unpleasant, current or distant—and gain clarity. Moreno called psychodrama "the theatre of the mind."

As you will learn as you read bits and pieces of my history contained within, and chronicled in more detail in "About the Author" near the end of the book, psychodrama helped me save my psychological life.

I was inspired to take an inner journey when, at about 40 years old, I received the phone call from hell, and my life came crashing down around me. That phone call signaled the end of my marriage, quite unexpectedly. That apparently cataclysmic event in my life turned out to be key to my own healing: Over time, and with the help of the practice of psychodrama, I realized I had been pretending to be who I thought other people wanted me to be, and I saw how destructive that had been for me. Through the continued practice of psychodrama, I took the opportunity to find out who I really am. Because of how psychodrama helped me change my life, I vowed to change careers and pass it on—which I have done.

All that said brings me back to this book, an effort to share with you a slice of the self-understanding the practice of psychodrama has gifted to me. My greatest hope for this humble work is that reading these stories and sayings in this context will be food for thought, at least. At best, I hope that this book will impart insights that will serve as touchstones along your own path of healing your inner child, so that you can live a more authentic, rich and wildly fulfilling life. Real really *is* better than perfect.

DOROTHY BALDWIN SATTEN, PhD

April 2006

On Authenticity

If you don't reveal yourself,
people will invent you—
and they'll always get it wrong.

When operating from authenticity,
there is no anxiety or guilt.
Anxiety is about the future;
guilt is about the past. Authenticity
is about the here and now.

Do what you do in life because
it's your passion, the authentic you.
Doing what is not you
will always bring pain.

If we want to be authentic, we must seek

the courage to bring our pain and fear

into the sunlight, leave it there,

and look at it.

We have to resist the urge to drag it

back into the dark.

If you must be "cool and cosmic"

—do it sparingly!

The idea of "selfishness" is overused in our society, and men and women who erase their needs and end up being unhappy are the result. There are some people who are true narcissists—they think of no one's needs but their own. But in most cases, what has been taught to us as being "selfish"—like taking time to meet our own needs—is really "self-care." Self-care is mandatory for living a satisfying life. Charity really does begin at home. And if you don't do self-care, no one gets much from you that's authentic.

Your inner child is your
first-born daughter, if you're a woman,
and son, if you're a man.
Your inner child will be with you
when you die. At the end of the day,
you'll want to have your integrity intact,
and your arm around that child.

The most important journey
you'll ever take is the one
between your head and your heart.

What I strive for in my life is authenticity.
I take inventory every night,
and I've never lived a perfect day.
So I've had to learn to forgive
myself over and over, because
real is better than perfect.

On Compassion

Compassion, like charity, begins at home. We have to forgive ourselves over and over again.

Through "role-reversing"—putting
yourself in someone else's skin—you learn
x-ray vision. This x-ray vision will
help you cultivate compassion for others
and, ultimately, for yourself.

See "X-Ray Vision," Appendix

If you can become the mother or father

that you wanted, you will be able

to be compassionate with your children—

and patient.

Bear in mind that the pain your
parents passed on to you, most likely,
was passed down to them first.
Imagining their lives, their parents'
lives, going back into history —
this is where compassion
for your parents begins,
and forgiveness.

Ask yourself some serious
questions, and slowly imagine the
answers: What would it be like
to have you as a girlfriend or boyfriend?
To be married to you?
To have you as a mother? A father?
Husband? Wife? Lover? A parent,
co-parent, or teenager? What would it be
like to be your little girl, or little boy?
An intellectual companion,

a traveling companion, a confidant, or a partner who shares financial responsibilities? A soul-searching mission to answer these questions will give you a different perspective. It will help you develop compassion for the people in your life, and to act accordingly. It's also key to developing compassion for yourself.

If we don't have compassion
for ourselves, we can't truly have
compassion for another person.

One of the most important things any
couple can do: Tell each other the story
of your journey in life up until you met—
not all at one time. When one speaks,
the other listens with no commentary.
This may take several evenings together.
Make it your passion to know your
partner's life; relationships with parents
and family members; ideas about truth,
privacy and responsibility; and feelings
about what has happened

in his or her life. The more you and
your partner know about each others' past,
the better you'll be at catching each other
"pasting faces" from the past
on one another, and knowing whose face
it really is and how to stop it! And the
more compassion you'll develop because
you understand where your partner
is coming from. Then you can help
to heal one another.

On Courage

Be true to who you really are,
and for this great courage, ultimately,
will come great reward.

*H*olding on to yourself takes courage.

Sometimes, courage means
keeping your mouth shut.

Courage, sometimes, means
speaking out loudly—surprising
yourself and others!

My son Fred has a son, Bolan.

Bolan is a special pal of mine, and since
I've had a stroke, he helps me up and down
the stairs at his house quite tenderly.
One day when Bolan was about 5 years old,
he helped me down the stairs, and at the
bottom, we sat down together.
He said to me, "You know, Grandma Dudya
[as he calls me], you're going to die soon."
Bolan was very serious. I answered him,

"Bolan, I'm not even sick.

Why do you think I'm going to die soon?"

Bolan looked at me very authoritatively,

his eyes watering, and said,

"Well, you've just had too many

birthdays!" Bolan was obviously

afraid of losing me, and possibly

quite soon. Sometimes courage means

speaking your truth and facing your

fears head-on.

My son, Fred, is a doctor. Early in his clinical training, a woman my age died in his arms. He called to tell me, and I asked him, "Fred, what did you do?"

He said, "Mom, I held her…. Then I slipped off into the ward laundry room where no one would see me as I wept, thinking that one day, it will be you. I don't know if I can do this." "Oh, but you must," I told him. "The day that I can't be moved by the suffering of my clients is the day I'll hang up my shingle."

Authenticity takes courage.

When hurtful things happened to us or
those around us as children, there was
nothing we could do but go
into survival mode.
As adults, we can revisit what happened
with wiser eyes. It takes courage to go
back to dark places, but revisiting
these events and rescuing that "child"
is what allows us to move
from understanding ourselves
to *knowing* ourselves—
the path to living fully.

No one has the right to abuse you.

Tell someone. Get help.

I have favorite posters. On one,

the moonlight is making

the dew drops on a beautiful tree

in the dark woods sparkle.

The caption reads,

"In the midst of winter, I finally learned

that there was within me

an invincible summer."

I believe that "invincible summer"

endures in all of us.

From a poem by Albert Camus
(1913-1960)

Love is as love does.
Living your love takes
true courage.

On Fear and Anger

Fear often masks anger, and anger often masks fear. Where I grew up, it wasn't safe to be afraid, so I learned to mask that fear with anger or false bravery. Now, when I feel the impulse to be angry, I try to catch myself in that split second before I turn into someone I don't respect. I ask myself what I'm afraid of. When I'm in a safe environment, I report the impulse to be angry, and I share what I'm afraid of instead— which is much more honest.

Be your own good detective. If you tend to get angry first, try to find out what you're afraid of. If you're often fearful, try to discover what you're angry about.

One day, Mort and I were visiting my daughter, Mary, and her family in Hong Kong. Anna Sophia, Mary's daughter, then age 3, came into the guest bedroom where Mort and I were staying, and asked me, "How long were you married to my other Grandpa?" I told her we had been married almost 20 years. She asked me, "How long have you been married to Grandpa Mort?" I told her 19 years. She then asked, "Are you going to get rid of Grandpa Mort

when it's been 20 years?" Looking over
at Mort only half-asleep next to me,
I answered, coyly, "Not if he's good!"
(Of course, I then made it clear to Anna that
I was just kidding, and that I was
not going to be leaving her Grandpa Mort.)
Anna apparently had some anxiety
about the future, and whether Mort
was going to be around. When she asked,
and I answered, it relieved her anxiety.
Don't be afraid to ask your questions.

Anger sits on love like fat

on a good soup.

I grew up on a ranch. There,

we used to take the soup outside

on the cold back porch and let the fat

harden on the top, then scrape it off.

With anger, you have to see it

and acknowledge that it's just

a cover for your fear.

Then you can get rid of it.

$\mathcal{O}\!\!\sim$

$\mathcal{A}$t any given time,

we are coming either from fear,

or from love. We have a choice.

Remember, there is such a thing

as ethical anger: against injustice,

prejudice, violence, corruption

in government and business,

betrayal, etc.

Based on the writings of Gerald Jampolsky.
See *Love is Letting Go of Fear*, "Recommended Reading."

My husband, Mort, had major surgery at the age of 80, and of course, I wondered if I would lose him. Mort survived the surgery—he's a heroic figure. But I found that I kept the fear alive by thinking of losing him. I was scaring myself. Of course, it's true that every one of us will die one day, and that each of us must prepare for that eventuality. What is unwise is to scare ourselves by future-tripping into dark places. In that way, the joyous opportunities of the moment become invisible to us, and our own life slips away.

Nothing is eaten as hot as it's cooked.

GERMAN PROVERB

Fear is instilled in us at an early age.

It splits us away from ourselves.

If the family a child is in makes them

fearful and causes them pain,

a child sometimes fantasizes that he

or she is in the wrong family.

You have to be willing to adopt yourself—

become your own good father,

your own good mother.

Life is full of surprises; be prepared

to do this many times.

On Forgiveness

Think of someone you don't forgive.
When we don't forgive, it's like dragging
that person around with you—
a body around one ankle.
The way to forgive the errors
of past relationships is to take
a very honest look at what went wrong,
and own your part of making things
go wrong: Every time you tell the truth
you honor yourself. Owning your
part is the beginning of forgiveness
and of setting yourself free.

*F*orgiveness happens in your heart.
You can decide to tell the person, or not.

You can make amends, or not.

Sometimes, another person won't accept

your forgiveness. What matters is that

you don't fail to forgive.

If you can't forgive yourself,
you'll arrange a punishing life
for yourself.
If you've arranged a punishing life
for yourself, it would be good to examine
what you think you're guilty of.

When I had a stroke at 65, I was angry
with myself—angry that I hadn't eaten
better, exercised more, rested more. I
wasn't sure if I could forgive myself.
I had to decide if I could add the stroke
to who I am, or if I would let it shrink me
to less than I am. Forgiving myself
was the first step in being able to add
that experience to who I am.
I practice *daily*.

One year during the holidays, Mort and I
were at our home and all the children
were visiting. My grandson, Nathaniel,
age 10, was upstairs playing a computer
game. When it came time to eat,
I called the family together,
wanting to get everyone to the table
while the food was still hot.
Nathaniel was slow to comply, so finally

Mort went to fetch him, losing his temper in the process. Mort's anger frightened Nathaniel. Later, Mort apologized and explained why he had gotten angry. Nathaniel forgave him openheartedly, and the relationship was undamaged. Today, the two are close.

It takes courage to apologize, and compassion to forgive.

We have to forgive ourselves
over and over and over again.

From Sheldon Kopf, psychiatrist, author

*F*orgiveness is one of the most underrated tools in mental health.

If you don't forgive,
a bitter heart is not
far behind.

On Friendship

A friend is someone who sees right
through you and likes the show.

True friends don't keep score—
they root for both of you to win.

Most of the events that have damaged us

happened behind closed doors

with *no* witnesses.

A friend listens and becomes your witness

so that you can begin to heal.

*I*f you have one friend
in your lifetime who knows your story,
you are truly blessed.

*C*lear boundaries make
for long friendships.

*F*riendship is often an underrated relationship. The psychologist/ psychodramatist Martin Haskell taught the concept of a "personal reference group." We don't get to choose our first families, but we do get to choose our personal reference group, including all of our friends. Those hand-selected sisters, brothers, aunts, uncles, mothers and fathers can become our supportive, healthy family.

If you isolate yourself
following tragic events in your life,
you deprive yourself of support
from loving friends.

One or two real friends are worth

hundreds of acquaintances.

Your friends are the ones who have helped enrich your life, and you have enriched theirs. They're the ones who will show up at your funeral—

unless they're dead!

True friends don't expect you to change,

but in some cases, they're awfully

glad when you do!

A true friend knows the meaning
of confidentiality, and they're with you,
rain or shine.

On Healthy Statements
and Questions

!?

*H*ow is your interior life?

*I*t's O.K. with me if you outgrow me.

Don't erase any part of yourself
to be what you think I want.

When you're behaving in a way
you don't respect, who from your past
gets to be right about you?
Or, who gets to be wrong about you?
Who's life is your life beginning
to look like, and is that O.K. with you?
Food for thought.

Does your well-being depend upon
remembering *every* little detail
and *every* single hurt of your life?
If it does, you've found a good excuse
for staying stuck.

You are not me.

You are not your mother.

You are not your father.

You are your own wildly unique person.

In all of history—for eons and eons—
there will never be another you.
You are unique in the universe!
Isn't that wonderful?

On Helplessness
and Rage

Helplessness and rage are a matched pair
(like fear and anger). When one is being
expressed, the other is there,
but unexpressed. To understand rage,
get in touch with how you feel helpless.

People believe that experiencing

their helplessness will be fatal—

so instead, they rage.

It takes a lot of helplessness

to cover up rage, and a lot of rage

to cover up helplessness.

$\mathcal{A}$ single mother with three teenage sons was raging at them whenever they seemed out of control.

It was not who she wanted to be.

She told me, "I don't understand what comes over me." What a courageous mother she was, wanting to stop something that was hurting her boys. I asked her to try to catch herself just before she blew her top, and instead, tell her boys how

helpless and sad she felt that she couldn't
be their mother and father both; and
instead of trying to hide, to let them see
her cry. She told me later that
admitting to her boys that she felt defeated
and helpless strengthened their relationship
tremendously. She hasn't raged since. No
one can control the universe. There is great
power in embracing your helplessness.

Rage is different from anger in that
it is not directed at anyone or anything
in particular. Behind all rage is a sense
of helplessness. For those who live
with a sense of rage, it is wise to locate
that helplessness—that event, or events,
that over time made you feel powerless
in your own life.
Getting in touch with the origin of that
wounding is a beginning step
in healing yourself of rage.

On Love —
Giving and Receiving

Real love means being the authentic you.

Real love cuts the partner some slack.

The best gift you can give
to your children—and to anyone else in
your life—is to model self-care.

Setting clear boundaries is a loving gift
to yourself and everyone else in your life.

Every time my mother and I would visit,

she would want to cook for me

or do my laundry. What I wanted was

to sit and talk like two intelligent

adult women. I was quite disappointed

and irritated that she couldn't seem

to love me like I wanted to be loved.

One day, I had the realization that

we were on different channels;

she was giving love on Channel 4,

and I was tuned to Channel 2,

wanting to receive there. I realized that

to receive her love, I needed to re-tune.
Some days after that realization, I arrived
at her home and asked enthusiastically
what she was cooking. I noticed there
was nothing cooking. To my utter shock
and disbelief, Mother said, "Forget about
cooking and the laundry! We're going out
to have dinner and talk like two adult
women!" This is an illustration of the truth
of the Buddhist saying, "After acceptance
comes change"—and never before.

Our integration of lessons learned is
always tested. Did I really get that lesson?
When my oldest son Robert died,
it was a tragedy I thought I wouldn't
survive; I had to pull myself out of his
grave many times. On one occasion,
my mother accompanied me to visit
Robert's grave. It was the dead of winter,
and the snow was a foot high.
As I approached the grave, overcome
with grief, I felt something pelt me
in the back of my head.

I turned around and spied my mother
in her bright red coat peeking out from
behind a gravestone and tossing another
snowball my way. At first I was
incredulous, wondering how my mother
could do such a thing. How could she be so
cold-hearted? At that moment I understood
the lesson of the channels; the snowballs
were her way of trying to pull me out of
my sorrow—her way of loving me.
When I switched to her channel,
I could receive her love.

You're always either coming
from love, or coming from fear.
When you're angry, most likely you're
coming from fear. When you have
the impulse to act angrily, ask yourself
instead what you're afraid of.
Share the answer, and you're
coming from love.

Based on the writings of Gerald Jampolsky.
See *Love is Letting Go of Fear*, "Recommended Reading."

It's hard to live a juicy adult life

when we've left parts of ourselves

in the school rooms, bedrooms, and dark

halls of the past. We reclaim those parts

when we can step outside and connect to

the wise person within, revisit those scenes,

and liberate the child we left behind.

We are then open to giving and receiving

love freely, with no hidden agenda.

We waste time when we wait
for a safe time to say our "I Love Yous."
There is no safe time...only Now.
It's all about what we do with the
Nows that we have.

On Parenting
and Patience

The greatest blessing in life
is having had healthy, grown-up parents.
If you weren't blessed with that, you can
heal childhood wounds
by becoming to *yourself* the parents
you always wanted.

The best thing you can do
for your children is to get a life that
doesn't revolve around them!

$\mathcal{F}$red, my youngest son, telephoned
me one day and told me this story.
He and his wife Elizabeth had been
building a fence in their backyard.
Their 6-year-old daughter, Pendle Faith,
was in the house with a friend sailing toy
boats in the upstairs bathroom sink. Then
the girls went on to other games. Some
time later, Pendle Faith came out to the
yard and said, "Daddy, it's raining in the
kitchen." Fred said, "Elizabeth and I threw
down our tools," both understanding that
the source of the downpour was the

boat party in the upstairs bathroom.
I asked Fred, "What did you do?" He said,
"I squatted down, took Pendle Faith's little
hands in mine, and said, 'Pendle, go
upstairs and lock yourself in your
bedroom!'" When Fred told me this story,
I knew I had done something right as a
parent. When I next visited the family,
Pendle asked me if I'd seen their new
kitchen. She told me that if she hadn't
made it rain, they'd still just have the
old one. Children have healthy ways of
re-framing. We can learn from them.

The wounded child within will often take the path of least resistance— what's familiar. Rather than taking the path of least resistance, why not take the path of greatest advantage? If what you're doing isn't working, give yourself permission to do things differently. Then have patience with yourself as you change.

My Italian grandmother Rachaela
said, "When you raise children,
be prepared to eat a barrel of salt."
When I raised my children, I was
careful how I spoke with them.
Salty words can hurt; best
to swallow them.

*I*n raising children, look for what they
do right, not what they do wrong.
Look for the one time they hang up their
jackets, or they come to the table having
washed their hands, or they tidy up
their rooms. Praise what they do right.
They want your love.

When clients have come to me, afraid
of what kind of parents they might be,
I always tell them, "Become the mother
you would have wanted, or the father
you would have wanted."
That's the secret of good parenting.

Something that helped me
after my son's death was knowing that
I really had gotten to know him, and had
allowed him to know me. Get to know
your children, and let them know the real
you; that makes for no regrets.

Decisions should not be rushed
to an end that could create regrets;
patience is golden. Not to be ready
to make a decision is a valid place
in a decision-making process.
When it's time, decisions
often make themselves.

People share what they're ready to share

and do what they're ready to do.

It's disrespectful to push.

Rather than disrespect,

I get to work on my patience.

When you've done wrong
by your children, you know it.
All parents know when they're
getting it wrong. When it's called for,
step up to the plate:
Apologize to your children,
ask for their forgiveness...
and shape up!

There are many ways privacy
can be invaded: Parents who don't
knock on doors before entering or ask
if it's a good time to talk; parents who
read diaries or go through dresser drawers
or pants pockets. Breaches of privacy in
childhood set us up for being lax or
overly rigid in setting our own
boundaries as adults.

Children should be taught the meaning
of confidentiality.
Practicing confidentiality
engenders trust.

If you never tell your children about any mistakes you've made, you do them a great disservice. They want to know that you're real, not perfect.

On Prisons
and Setting Yourself Free

There are many kinds of prisons—not trusting men, or women; not having enough leisure time, feeling unworthy, feeling as though we have to do twice as good to get half as far... Those who are imprisoned young will seek out the same prison later because they already have the tools to survive there. So as children we become 'survivors;' then, during our lives, recreate the circumstances with which we are familiar and can cope. Each of us must explore how we are wounded before we can learn to thrive, rather than just survive.

If you've arranged a punishing life
for yourself, it would be well to explore
what you feel you're guilty of.

Failing to take actions important
for our own lives and our own
happiness, just because we imagine
others may disapprove, is the
hero's way to hell.

We all know when a well is dry.

Every family I've ever known has its

dry-well member (or members).

It makes no sense to go to a dry well

to get a drink and then curse

the well because it's dry.

All behavior is designed,
on some level, to elicit exactly
the response it gets.

We treat ourselves the way we
were treated as children. If we were
never listened to, we don't listen
to ourselves as adults.

When we can identify ways
we were mistreated, we can decide
if that's how we want to continue
to treat ourselves. Sometimes we have
to give ourselves permission
to outgrow our parents.

Mental health begins
when there's no one left to blame.

MORT SATTEN

I began to get well when I got bored

of hearing my own war stories.

For some people, it's unfamiliar
to feel good. So when they begin to feel
good, they'll run right back
to the feel-bad place. We all know
how to feel miserable. The challenge
sometimes is allowing yourself
to feel good.

One value of mine is to be fair.

How I've lost 12 pounds:

Reminding myself that if I overeat,

I'm eating more than my fair share

of the world's food!

No one I've ever known
has escaped having negative behaviors.
From time to time it can be instructive
to look at those behaviors that are
not good for us, like overeating,
overworking, drinking too much.
Understanding who they keep us connected
to, and who they make right about us,
is a first step in breaking free.

The moment we feel scared,
the wounded child within will want
to run back to where she was imprisoned
because it's familiar. Our job is to head
her off at the pass ... and to love
and comfort her.

When something doesn't work,

many of us just do it louder.

If you do what you've always done,

you'll get what you always got.

So try something different!

From the teachings of Dr. Carl Hollander
Gifted Therapist, Teacher, Friend and Mentor

If you're angry, look angry—don't smile.
Otherwise, you betray yourself and your
true feelings. And, people don't take you
seriously when there's no congruence.
Doing our emotions clearly and
honestly we keep our self-respect
and set ourselves free.

Wanting more for someone
than they want for themselves
is the royal road
to burnout.

I once had a patient who seemed
to be holding on to his anger and
disappointment. I asked him what it was
going to take for him to get well. He told
me it was going to take lots of time and
money, because if he recovered quickly,
his parents wouldn't know how badly they
had screwed him up. I realized that he was
willing to give up his mental health
to punish his parents. We need
to make sure that we're not holding on
to pain to punish someone else.

*I*t's important to ask yourself
from time to time where you're headed
if you don't change anything, and if that's
OK. Otherwise, you'll never know if you
need to change directions. If you keep on
going in the same direction, you'll
end up where you're headed.

It's a trap to live our lives based on
what we think "they" will think;
first, because it's impossible
to know what they'll think.
Second, we end up not living
an authentic life, but living
someone else's life.

Matthew, Mark, Luke, John, and They.
"What will *They* say?" Too often we run
our lives out of that Fifth Gospel—
the Gospel According to "They."

MORT SATTEN

On Relationship

Years after the end of my first marriage
I realized why we had no chance to turn
our difficult issues into our growing edge:
We never talked about what we
never talked about.

*I*f we don't reveal ourselves,
others invent us. Instead of falling
in love with a real person, they fall
in love with their invention of us,
or we, with our invention of them—
and both are wrong. Authenticity

goes out the window.

Reveal yourself!

You know when you're growing
in real love when, instead of loving
someone "in spite of" their little flaws,
you come to realize you love them
because of those flaws.

*C*odependence is when you're dying
and someone *else's* life passes
before your eyes!

*I*nterdependence is like corn and beans
planted together; the beans replace what
the corn needs and takes from the soil, and
the corn provides the stalk for the beans to
climb up. They share the same sunlight and
rain. It's not competitive, but mutual and
reciprocal. And it's what you want
in a relationship.

You can create intimacy with another human being only to the extent that you can "role-reverse" with that person.

See "X-Ray Vision," Appendix

*I*t is well to role-reverse,

and to do it often. We can do this

by answering, honestly, questions like,

"What would it be like to be my friend?

My son? My daughter? My husband

or wife? My lover?" When we have the

courage to answer those questions and

to see where we're getting it wrong,

we then have the opportunity

to get it right.

When two people in a relationship
don't honor their own needs first, but
instead, try to become what they guess will
please their partner, they erase themselves.
Both end up unhappy. Honor your partner;
don't expect them to read your mind—tell
the truth about what you need. Be
your authentic self!

To have a healthy relationship, everyone needs to know first how to be happy with themselves—take time to explore their own needs and "get their arms around themselves." When you're looking for a life partner, look for a person who recognizes their own needs and takes care of himself or herself—a person with their arms around themselves. If you're looking for someone to take care of and make happy, or someone to take care of you and make you happy, you're a train wreck waiting to happen.

If you marry for passion,
don't expect a housekeeper!

*I*n an intimate adult relationship,

don't turn yourself into the child

or the parent. Doing either is the kiss

of death in terms of maintaining

intimacy.

A relationship is about relating.
You can create a relationship only
with someone you spend time with.

I once interviewed a woman to be my assistant. She told me: "I will always be on time and will work from 9 to 5, and never a minute more. I will not shop for office supplies, but I'll leave you a list of what I need. And I will always keep work confidential."

Well, I wasn't sure how such a

relationship would work out—

I had a bad habit of asking my assistants

to stay longer and do little extras...

Because of this woman's boundaries and

excellent work, it turned out we had a

great working relationship.

Good boundaries make for

great relationships.

You never have more leverage
in a relationship than at the beginning
when the ground rules are established.
It's always easier to give up ground
later than it is to take back ground
you've given up at the beginning.
Stand your ground!

Ninety-nine-point-nine percent
of what other people are saying or doing
is about them. Best not waste time
worrying that it's about you.

My husband, Mort, and I were driving together one day, and I was wearing a new coat. He turned to me and said, "I see that's a new coat you're wearing." The tone of his voice led me to believe he was irritated, and I had the impulse to justify the purchase of the coat—to tell him that, in fact, it was a new coat purchased with my own money. But I knew that if I did, it would end in a ruckus. Instead, I decided to report my impulse, and said, "Yes it is a new coat, and I have the impulse to defend its purchase."

After a few moments of silence, to my surprise, Mort replied, "It's difficult for me to give myself new things." I felt closer to him after he said that. I then told him I had never had new clothes as a child; my aunt had sent hand-me-downs. We spent five or ten minutes sharing with each other about the feelings we had surrounding giving to ourselves. Reporting our impulses, rather than acting upon them, can open up opportunities for true intimacy.

You'll know you're ready for the love of your life when you've become the person you'd like to be with.

On Risk and
Success

To not risk anything is to risk everything.

We create our lives based on what we
believe are our possibilities.

What we believe are our possibilities

has a lot to do with what we were told

about ourselves when we were children.

It's good to examine those messages...

You just might disagree!

There is nothing quite as sad
as living a dead life by playing it safe
all the time and just "going along."

We don't learn anything from our safe, familiar place. We learn when we dare to explore the unknown.

"On the plains of hesitation

Bleach the bones

of countless thousands

Who at the dawn of victory,

sat down to wait

And waiting, died."

GEORGE W. CECIL
American Magazine
March 1923

I have a friend who has written
songs since she was 11 years old.
For years she compared her songs
to the songs of others—and of course,
in her mind, her songs never quite
measured up. One day, her desire
to share herself became greater than
her fear of not measuring up; she
stopped comparing and threw

caution to the wind. She recorded

20 songs in a studio in Nashville,

and today, hundreds of thousands

of people have been inspired

by her music. If she had continued

comparing, she could never have

come this far. Measure yourself only

against your own known best.

You can't create anything in your life

unless you can imagine it.

Nothing turns out exactly as we think it will—and that's good to remember.

It doesn't matter
where you start, just that
you start.

If you're walking on thin ice,

you may as well dance!

A saying from my father,
Oä Cecil Baldwin

When what you know in your heart
and believe to your core is threatened—
and you stand by and do nothing—
there is nothing quite as disempowering
or as deeply sad. Stand up for what you
believe, and you will become
the person you were intended to be.

On Self-Care

*I*t's an illusion to think that

you are giving anything really authentic

to others if you are not being

true to yourself.

Self-care is where loving kindness

must start to be authentic.

We've been bamboozled into believing
that it's selfish to take care of our own
needs, when in fact, that's where
all authentic caring begins.
For many of us who grew up
with role models of moms who lived
only to meet the kids' needs,
and dads who were workaholics who
never took time for themselves, "selfish"
must be reframed to "self-care."

It is important to create time to take care of our physical health. How well we're doing with that can also be a window into the state of our mental heath. After my son Robert died, I put on a good 20 pounds or so right in front; I actually looked pregnant. I realized one day that extra weight kept me bonded to the idea of motherhood, and to the memory of Robert. When I realized that I didn't need to look pregnant to be a mother, or to remember Robert, I was able to take those extra pounds off.

It's not loving to allow anyone
in your life to abuse you. Setting clear
boundaries, self-care, is the loving thing
to do. That way, people know where
they stand with you, and more important,
you know where you stand with yourself.

*I*t was Christmas eve in Hong Kong. My daughter, Mary, was negotiating the traffic, and I was her front-seat passenger. Everybody in Hong Kong seemed to be out looking at Christmas lights.

In the back in his car seat sat Mary's youngest son Benjamin, age 2, with a little friend. The two had been enjoying seeing all the pretty lights, but it was late, and both were beginning to get fussy. At one point, the two began to quarrel.

Mary tried to intervene and coax Ben
to "be nice" to his little friend, even though
she understood he was very tired. After
a number of well-meant directives from
his mother, Ben finally said firmly,

"I don't want to, and, I don't
want to want to!' Benjamin knew exactly
what he wanted and didn't want—
on several levels. Self-care means
knowing what you want
and expressing it.

*I*t's challenging to hold on to yourself.

We'll all die someday, but there's no need to go prematurely because of lack of self-care. If I die, where will my spirit live? And besides, I'm having too much fun...

MORT SATTEN, AGE 81

One of the ways I practice self-care is to have talks with myself from time to time—just to make sure I'm going in the right direction, since that's where I'm going to end up! To talk to myself, I put something in a chair to represent me as I am now, and I back away from that chair a year, two years, three—all the way to the place that represents the last day of my life. From that place of wisdom, I look back at myself in the chair, today; I tell Dorothy how I feel about her, and what I want

for her in that distance between where
she is now, and the last day of her life—
like getting exercise daily, being more
patient with herself and what she is unable
to do since the stroke, spending more time
with her family. I also tell her what I want
her to guard against—like getting
overtired, gaining weight back, feeling
overwhelmed… It's amazing the advice
Wise Dorothy has for Dorothy from that
position. I find it to be an extremely valuable
exercise for getting on the right track.

No one says on the last day
of their life that they regret not having
spent more time at the office.

On Sex

Sex is meant to be loving, nourishing,

tender...and fun! Sex should never

be used as a weapon for control,

or for causing pain.

Withholding sex or demanding sex
are two sides of the same
problem: control.

If you turn your partner into your parent,

or a child, sex will go out the window.

If you allow your partner to turn you

into their parent or a child,

sex goes out the window. Why?

Because in our culture,

incest is forbidden, and sex

is for consenting adults! Similarly,

a loving and authentic marriage can only

be worked out by grown-ups.

Real love-making is possible
when partners give themselves permission
to talk freely about things that are difficult
to talk about, and really listen to one
another—and want to know.
It happens when partners appreciate the
little things they do for each other and say
to each other every day. The intimacy born
of the talking, listening, and appreciating
turns sex into real love-making.

Sex can take place for many reasons,

which is no new news to most of us,

I'm sure. Real love-making is sex

and so much more—

it's a joyous expression of intimacy.

*I*t's important that couples ask each other
what they learned from their parents
about sex. What did their mother think
about sex? Their father? Did they see any
affection pass between the parents?
Did the parents snuggle or dance together?
What each person in the couple
learned growing up sets the stage
for their attitudes about sex.

To have a healthy sex life, both partners
must get their parents, and their parents'
views on sex, out of the bedroom!
It's difficult to have an intimate, fulfilling
experience with six in the bed!

No going to bed mad—ever.

No teasing about the body—it's not fair.

Sex is in the mind!

Personally, I think there should be

a lot of laughter in the bedroom.

Sex in a healthy relationship,
where both people have their arms around
themselves, and there is intimacy and trust,
is like a fine glass of wine:
it gets better with age.

Sex is a beautiful thing.
I think of it as a gift of spirit,
a window into heaven—into our
vulnerable, childlike, passionate
and most real selves.
Share it wisely.

On Therapy

You can't get to your ecstasy
until you've gotten to your agony.

Therapy is not life.

Life is life.

You know what you need
better than any therapist.
The best therapist in the world for you
is the therapist inside.
Listen.

*T*herapy that tries to control,

or tell you what to do, is not good therapy;

it's just replacing one set of controls

external to yourself with another.

All good therapy is re-parenting—

the therapist simply becomes a good

role model and encourages you

to discover your authentic self.

I started to get well when I got

tired of my old, sad story.

*M*ental illness is not knowing what you

want and busting your buns to get it!

Mort Satten

*A*ll of us are therapists to those in our lives, and in that role, we are either toxic, or generative. The best insurance against being "toxic" and hurting others is working on your own unfinished business.

The purpose of therapy is not for the therapist to give you all the answers—the truth is, he or she doesn't know them. All that therapy can hope to accomplish is to shorten the lag time between suffering and becoming yourself.

During a very difficult period in my life,

I was blessed with a wonderful therapist.

One day I felt so down, I just couldn't

drive the 20 miles to his office. I called

and said, "I don't think I can make it

today; I won't be coming." He replied,

"I'll be waiting for you in the parking lot.

I'll take my folding chair and newspaper

down there and wait for you."

Then he hung up. I called him back.

There was no answer. I tried several more

times, and nothing! I thought, "Surely

he wouldn't sit down there waiting

for me?" But I had to be sure.

So I drove those 20 miles. There he was

in the parking lot. He said to me,

"I knew you could do it, and I

wanted *you* to know you could do it."

He then said, "There's no charge for this

visit. You can drive back home now."

Someone who really believes in you can be

of such help and healing.

Michelangelo was chatting
with a group of young sculptors one day
near a marble quarry, all of them waiting
for the next chunks of marble to arrive.
He had been working on what some
thought was the most exquisite sculpture
of a horse ever created. This day,
the group was singing the praises of that
sculpture-in-progress while
simultaneously lamenting their
lack of mastery of sculpting
compared to Michelangelo's.

"How is it that you are so prolific, and
your work is so consistently inspired?"
asked one young sculptor, quite perplexed.
Michelangelo looked over to where the next
load of marble would soon arrive, thought
for a moment, then replied: "I don't wait
for the perfect piece of marble," he said.
"Rather, I take the very next piece that is
available, with all its flaws, and simply get
rid of everything that is not my horse."
Good therapy helps us get rid of everything
that is not our horse.

My oldest son, Robert, died at 24.

On the mornings when I wake up

remembering him, a wave of sorrow

overtakes me. I could fixate on that loss.

Or ...

I can swing my legs out of bed,

be deeply grateful for another day,

and show up for myself and

the people in my life.

We can let sorrows drown us—

the memories of our failures,

how people have hurt us,

who we've lost.

Or ...

we can look to the glory of the day

and resurrect ourselves.

Now *that's* therapy!

*D*uring a difficult period,
I entered therapy for one year.
During my last session, the therapist
asked what had been most valuable.
I shared two things: One day, she had
put her hand on my shoulder and had
reassured me that everything would be
all right. Another day, she had put on her
winter boots and helped me dig my car
out of the snow. Small acts of humanity
can be the most powerful therapy.

On Truth

Mahatma Gandhi was teaching one day,
and a woman in the crowd said to him,
"But Gandhiji, what you're saying today is
not what you said before!" Gandhi replied,
"Madame, it is not my aim to speak the
truth as I may have spoken it on a previous
occasion, but to move from truth to truth,
and speak the truth as I now know it."
Let yourself move from truth to truth.

—FROM THE TEACHINGS OF MAHATMA GANDHI

Using your truth to hurt others
diminishes you—and your truth.

I'm more afraid of bitterness
than of dying. The bitter heart can soften
by remembering the love.
To heal yourself from bitterness,
you must tell yourself the truth
about your part of what made things
go wrong in a relationship.

In Hemingway's book *Islands in the Stream*,
the hero had been troubled and puzzled
about how his family broke up and whose
fault it was. He is a gunrunner, and in the
end has been shot and lies dying in his boat.
He says aloud, "No one thing is true.
It's all true."
Something I've understood only recently
is that many things can be true
all at the same time.

You have to know

where you stand before

you can jump.

The truth really will set you free.
That's because being your real,
authentic self—finding and living
the truth you know in your heart
of hearts—is true freedom.

A favorite poster of mine features an old, gray, upright washing machine with a roller-wringer exactly like the Maytag we had on the back porch at the ranch.

In the poster, a Raggedy-Ann doll is halfway through the wringer. The caption says, "The truth will set you free. But first, it will piss you off!" When we finally find our truth, it's not always easy to face.

On Wounding
and Healing

When your well-being is external to you,
you are in a very vulnerable position—
it's a crapshoot. When you stop allowing
your well-being to depend on what
someone else does or doesn't do,
you begin to heal yourself.

If you're waiting for someone else
to understand you perfectly before
you're O.K., lots of luck!

Small shifts can create big changes in your life. Sit with your knees together, your feet flat on the floor, and look out in the distance at what's directly ahead of you. Now move your feet just slightly to the right or left, adjust your body so you're straight, and note how much what is directly ahead has changed—it's a big difference. It doesn't take a large shift in the tectonic plates of your psyche to make a great difference in where you'll end up in the distance. It can be as small as a slight shift in your attitude—and your whole life changes.

When parents lose a child,

in their grief, they may have the impulse

to "go into the grave" with that child and

stay there. Many families have been

abandoned by parents who do this.

Everyone is entitled to their own death.

We respect the life and memory of our

loved ones by not crawling into that grave

with them and abandoning the living.

I collected all of Robert's things after he
died and kept them in a trunk in the attic.
From time to time I would take myself
up there and look through his effects and
all the photos and letters, and
I would weep. I did this for quite some
time, like a ritual I had to do.
One day, I started up those stairs,
and I said to myself,

Better an ending with misery

than misery without end.

A German Saying

*I*t's not possible to have a different past,
so we might as well accept our own history.
We don't, however, have to drag those
ghosts around. When the will to know
finally overcomes the fear of knowing,
then we can begin dealing with the ghosts
one by one and start to heal our lives.

"You know exactly how you're going
to feel if you keep going up these stairs.
I'm not going to do that to you anymore—
no more picking at that scab."
I turned around and walked down the
stairs, and made myself a cup of tea.
Although I still think of my son often,
I now honor him specifically
on his birthday, and the day of his death.

People sometimes say they've thrown
someone they've loved out of their lives:
"Good riddance to bad rubbish."
It's best not to throw away someone
you've loved. When we do that,
we throw away a little piece of our own
hearts, and we delay our own healing.

On Truth

*Mahatma Gandhi was teaching one day,
and a woman in the crowd said to him,
"But Gandhiji, what you're saying today is
not what you said before!" Gandhi replied,
"Madame, it is not my aim to speak the
truth as I may have spoken it on a previous
occasion, but to move from truth to truth,
and speak the truth as I now know it."
Let yourself move from truth to truth.*

—From the teachings of Mahatma Gandhi

Using your truth to hurt others
diminishes you—and your truth.

I'm more afraid of bitterness
than of dying. The bitter heart can soften
by remembering the love.
To heal yourself from bitterness,
you must tell yourself the truth
about your part of what made things
go wrong in a relationship.

In Hemingway's book *Islands in the Stream*,

the hero had been troubled and puzzled

about how his family broke up and whose

fault it was. He is a gunrunner, and in the

end has been shot and lies dying in his boat.

He says aloud, "No one thing is true.

It's all true."

Something I've understood only recently

is that many things can be true

all at the same time.

You have to know
where you stand before
you can jump.

The truth really will set you free.
That's because being your real,
authentic self—finding and living
the truth you know in your heart
of hearts—is true freedom.

A favorite poster of mine features an old, gray, upright washing machine with a roller-wringer exactly like the Maytag we had on the back porch at the ranch.

In the poster, a Raggedy-Ann doll is halfway through the wringer. The caption says, "The truth will set you free. But first, it will piss you off!" When we finally find our truth, it's not always easy to face.

You have the Right to Be Here. You have the Right to Need, and to Separate and Be Yourself. You have the Right to Autonomy with Support, to Speak Your Own Truth, and the Right to a Passionate Adult Life. You have the Right to Find and Follow Your Own Spiritual Path. And you have the Right to Your Own Death. These rights don't have to be earned, but are our birthrights. Understanding them is key to discovering where we were wounded. Reclaiming these rights is key to healing our lives.

From *Character Styles*, by Stephen M. Johnson, one of my most beloved books. I added the last two Rights.

When I was a child I found a beautiful
Ponderosa pine in a clearing not far from
the ranch house. It was tall and sturdy, and
I loved to wrap my arms around its thick
trunk. When there was trouble in the house,
I used to visit that tree and hold it tight.
I would imagine that my roots went deep
into the earth, that my branches stretched
high into the sky, and that families of birds
found shelter there. That tree was my place
of refuge, where I felt safe, and I loved it
like a trusted friend. As an adult, I returned

to visit that tree. To my horror, I found that it had been struck by lightning. Splayed in two, blackened and devoid of foliage, I was sure that it was dead, and on that day, I wept. Several years later, I decided to visit that tree just one more time; I thought I would say goodbye. I walked solemnly to the clearing expecting to find it in a state of decay, disappearing back into the earth. But to my delight and amazement, in fact, there it stood: Where it had been split and blackened,

hearty, green shoots now grew up
and were nearly as tall as I! I recognized
that the life story of that old friend was
a powerful metaphor for my own life,
and for our lives:
Life, like lightning, splits open our hearts,
testing us to our core. From the ashes
of our pain and sorrow, new life
and hope spring forth.

Other Juicy Tidbits

I've come to learn that the high moral ground is extremely slippery.

Whenever I was kicked,
I was kicked up—although
I didn't realize it at the time.
When you feel you've been kicked,
pause; sit with your sadness and
grieve the hurt and loss.
When you're ready, think of what
you've learned: How did this cause you
to get unstuck or grow? In what other
way may it have been a gift? Then you'll
understand how you've been
kicked *up*.

Measuring yourself only against
your own known best will spare you
from the black hole of envy.

Anger, sadness, confusion...
It's not our feelings that trouble us,
it's how we feel about feeling them.

No one has the right to know everything about you, and you don't have the right to know everything about them. There are things we are entitled to keep to ourselves and take to our graves— and we should all reserve that right.

If you don't change directions,
you'll end up where you're headed.

*L*ife sends wake-up calls:

Finding true love, becoming a parent,

a narrow escape, a serious illness,

the death of a friend.

Don't sleep through the alarm!

If you don't think you can
change or learn anything new—
you're right.

We change our lives from what we really

come to *know* and *integrate*.

You may have twenty books on your

bookshelf about losing weight,

and from them, you'll gain lots of insight—

you'll understand all about losing weight.

You'll know you've really integrated those

insights, though, when you're thinner!

Until then, it's just blah, blah, blah …

You have to do what you have to do

as long as you have to do it.

Then you stop doing it.

We treat ourselves the way we were treated—and it's never too late to question if that's how we wish to continue.

We have to give ourselves permission
to live juicier lives than our parents did—
to outgrow them.

We're always teaching people
how to treat us.

I've never met a baby

with low self-esteem.

I've understood, only recently, that many things can be true at the same time.

Always do the next right thing.

MORT SATTEN

The map is not the terrain.

We know our path by walking it.

Let yourself move from truth
to truth in life.

FROM THE TEACHINGS OF MAHATMA GANDHI

"*If* at first you don't succeed,

try, try again," goes the proverb.

But if what you're doing isn't working,

don't do more. Wake up and

do something different!

Mort Satten

Be careful what you ask for—

you might just get it.

ORIGIN UNKNOWN

Love comes in many ways.
Become expert at recognizing
how you are being loved.

No power in this world can take away your innocence. You came into this world with it, and you'll leave with it.

Real is better than perfect!

*D*OROTHY BALDWIN SATTEN DID much of her growing up in Colorado. "I thought it was the whole world," Dorothy recalls of her grandfather's ranch, nestled in the heart of the Rockies amid thick, pine woodlands and tall mountains. During summers at the ranch she lived with grandparents on her mother's side and a gaggle of great aunts and uncles. Growing up with a maternal family of expressive Italians, "Doety," as they called her, became quite expressive herself and a colorful storyteller, as demonstrated by the short stories and inspiring "Dorothyisms" herein.

Little Doety excelled at writing and history in school, and was a precocious child. She remembers life on the ranch fondly, overall, especially her time alone in the fragrant forest where she would wish that she had come from a 'perfect family'—one where her parents never fought, always listened to her and her brother, and always gave wise advise. It was on one such occasion that, just behind her childhood home, Dorothy picked out a particularly old and large Ponderosa pine, "a wise one," she imagined, that she would put her arms around and hide in when "all hell was breaking loose" at the house. This happened rather frequently, since Dorothy's father, when drinking, could be a destructive man.

Dorothy's mother was a stylish and handsome woman with a ready sense of humor Dorothy credits with fueling her own razor wit. But she didn't offer much advice, usually insisting that Dorothy would "know when to come home" and know other things that a young girl shouldn't be expected to know. "I was always making up curfews for myself," Dorothy recalls of her life in grade school when it seemed other children had guidance that she lacked.

Her mother, who had no experience with alcoholism, was unable to buffer the children from their father. When he was in an alcoholic rage, she was terrified; he was loud, angry, mean and frightening to behold.

It was a household where little Doety had to be brave to protect her mother and brother; she learned that it wasn't safe to be afraid. And so, she learned to get angry—a reaction to fear she's had to practice long and hard to overcome. Now, as a septuagenarian, Dorothy says, "When I feel angry, I try to stop and think about what I'm afraid of."

Despite the chaos at home, young Doety, like all children, loved her father—"the sober father," she says now in hindsight. "Many of us had parents with two distinct personalities. I had 'two' fathers, one sober, and one alcoholic. It would do us well to be able to run our lives out of what we learned from the healthy side of our parents' personalities.

"We often find ourselves living out of the war stories and the horrors we experienced. My first mentor in the practice of psychodrama, Dr. Carl Hollander, asked me once, 'Besides being a brutal drunk, who else was your father?' I began to get well when I remembered who else my father was—that he had patiently spent long hours teaching me how to read before I entered first grade; that he played the guitar, he sang in Spanish—and he told wonderful stories. When I remembered my father's gifts, the rest of the truth, I began to heal. Over the years I also realized the many gifts my mother had given me, including patience, a love of life, and generosity, among the greatest."

When Dorothy was just 14, her father left the family. A few days later, her mother gave birth to Dorothy's youngest brother and went into a depression that necessitated that Dorothy grow up quickly. She had always wanted to become a doctor, but the expense dictated that medical school was not a possibility. At 18, Dorothy entered college as a pre-med student on scholarship;

she loved her studies, did cancer research, but had to leave the program due to finances. She later majored in history.

At 21, while still in school, Dorothy married a young medical student. Within several years, the two began a family. Robert was born first, followed by Mary, then Fred. While an attentive mother and a traditional stay-at-home wife, Dorothy went on to earn a credential and to become a teacher of ancient and medieval history. By all accounts, Dorothy was a "Superwoman" long before the term was coined.

The first inkling Dorothy had that her marriage of 19 years was in trouble was when her husband came up behind her one evening and whispered in her ear, "The problem with our relationship is that we're both in love with the same person—*me*." At the time, Dorothy thought the comment to be quite curious, since she had no conscious clue that their marriage was in trouble.

The following week, the marriage ended. At age 40, Dorothy's life was at a turning point: "I knew that all the things I had imagined for my future would never happen." Dorothy fell into a depression that lasted two years.

It wouldn't be until many years later that Dorothy would realize how thin her veil of happiness had been in that marriage—how she had "imported" her mother's fear of being deserted and had "erased" herself so she could try to be everything that her husband wanted her to be, and avoid her mother's fate. Ultimately, Dorothy experienced desertion as her mother had; and coincidentally, Dorothy's husband left when their daughter was 14—the same age Dorothy had been when her father left.

As Dorothy is now fond of saying, "Whenever I thought I had been kicked down in life, it always turned out that I had been kicked up," and that particular "kick" turned out to be an especially poignant gift—a wake-up call to get real with her life.

Dorothy knew that her former husband had referred a number of patients to an action therapy method called "psychodrama," and she decided to investigate it. That decision "saved my psychological life," she describes.

For the purpose of personal therapy, Dorothy began attending psychodrama, a form of group therapy wherein action is used to explore the painful places where wounding has taken place. "We've all left parts of ourselves in rooms, hallways, at summer camp, in dark alleys," Dorothy often explains to psychodrama groups. "Psychodrama is not designed to change you, but to help you go back for those parts so you can reclaim who you were meant to be—who you really are."

Psychodrama is a form of group therapy, where, within the safety of a pact of confidentiality, members of the group take on roles from the life of the protagonist, or "star" of a particular psychodrama. "Many of us were wounded in private, behind closed doors and without witnesses," Dorothy tells students. "In psychodrama, we have witnesses—people who are advocates, and are listening. It is a safe place where we can experience the situation from a different perspective and heal."

Dorothy studied psychodrama beginning in 1972. In 1974, she went to Beacon, the world-renowned Moreno Institute founded by Jacob Levy Moreno, the father of psychodrama, and his gifted wife, Zerka. Among psychotherapy greats who studied at Beacon were Fritz Perls who, based upon the Moreno method, developed Gestalt therapy; and Eric Berne, creator of transactional analysis and author of *The Games People Play*. Carl Hollander, a well-known psychotherapist and author, had also studied at the Moreno Institute and was among Dorothy's most trusted and helpful mentors.

In 1974, Dorothy married Mort Satten, a successful businessman and father of three teenagers, bringing their total combined teenagers to six, ages 13-18 (a perfect training ground for practicing marriage and family therapy!). Dorothy became a credentialed Marriage and Family Therapist and went into private practice specializing in psychodrama therapy for individuals and couples. She founded the Westwood Institute for Psychodrama and Psychotherapy in 1975 (the Ponderosa pine that was the place of refuge of her youth became the Institute's logo). Dorothy later earned a Ph.D. in clinical psychology.

Mort later returned to school and earned a Master's Degree in Marriage and Family Therapy, then joined Dorothy as a co-therapist in a successful practice. He earned a Ph.D. at the age of 65. They practiced in California until 2002, when they relocated the Westwood Institute to Tucson, Arizona.

Through the years, psychodrama remained Dorothy's passion. Besides it being integral to her therapeutic technique, she dedicated her life to passing on this powerful healing art. She and Mort held dozens of workshops for personal and professional growth each year worldwide. In April 2006, Dorothy received the J.L. Moreno Award from the American Society of Group Psychotherapy and Psychodrama for lifetime achievement.

Update, 2018 Edition:

Mort Satten passed away in 2009, followed by Dorothy in 2013. Through the many thousands of students and clients they helped to heal over decades, and the many therapists they trained, their legacy of love lives on.

J.L. Moreno Award, ASGPP

*I*n April 2006, the month of publication of this book's first edition, the American Society of Group Psychotherapy and Psychodrama bestowed upon Dorothy Satten the J. L. Moreno Award for Lifetime Achievement for her excellence, service and contributions to the field of psychodrama. Zerka Toeman Moreno, co-creator of psychodrama, contributed a version of the following letter to the proceedings:

> The J. L. Moreno Award presented to Dorothy Baldwin Satten is richly deserved. When Dorothy came to the Moreno Institute in 1974, neither Jacob nor I could have predicted how far she would carry on the work whose studies she had then just embarked upon.
>
> I used to say to the students: "Become a psychodramatist and see the world." Dorothy Satten did just that, and it is because of her steadfast and splendid work that the healing powers of psychodrama were brought to the attention of people far and wide.
>
> In March of 2006, Dorothy had the honor of being the first visiting trainer to present the J. L. Moreno Series at his very own theater in Highland, New York under the auspices of the Hudson Valley Psychodrama Institute. It is the same valley where Jacob Moreno grew his roots, and of which Dorothy Satten and Westwood Institute is one of the branches.
>
> Long may she thrive.

Zerka Toeman Moreno
April 2006

The American Society of Group
Psychotherapy and Psychodrama (ASGPP)
www.asgpp.org

COLLABORATOR'S NOTE

*I*t had been nearly a year since my husband and I had, after an eight-year run, indelicately ended our marriage. I was struggling to understand what had gone wrong. While I was tempted to blame it all on him, I knew I'd played a significant role in the failure, but I wasn't clear about what my part had been. I wanted to understand what was driving my fears and behaviors that had been destructive in the relationship. I knew that if I didn't address my issues then, I'd be doomed to repeat the pattern.

About this time, I was sharing the dismal story with a friend, Abdi Sami. While I had largely relied on instincts to slash a path ahead, Abdi had nurtured the good habit of seeking help to guide him through life's rough patches, and was stunningly self-aware because of it. His examined life had earned him a deep understanding and compassion for others that I couldn't help but notice. He stood out.

Abdi told me he owed much of his insight to his work with "two extraordinary therapists." He admired them both for the very effective work they did, and also, because of the deeply caring and kind people they were. The couple lived in Tucson, Arizona, he told me, but traveled the world sharing their healing craft through workshops in psychodrama—a powerful, action-method of therapy.

Abdi and I had our conversation on a Thursday, and as fate or fortune would have it, Dorothy and Mort Satten were conducting a psychodrama training near my home in Los Angeles that very weekend. On a dare to myself (I was not at all fond of the idea of pursuing personal growth in a group setting), I signed up for that two-day psychodrama workshop. Within the first hour of the first day, Dorothy said, "You have to get to your agony before you can get to your ecstasy." I remember thinking to myself, *Well, I'm at least halfway to my ecstasy!* That weekend was a bit of both, and it profoundly changed my life for the better.

Under Dorothy and Mort's guidance, and because of my willingness to explore the inner unknown, I was able to begin to unravel a lifetime of coping habits that were hindering my ability to be authentic in relationships, and were equally unhelpful in the broader context of my life. During the next several years, I traveled to dozens of Satten workshops and completed more than 400 hours of psychodrama training. I earned the title of Associate Director of Psychodrama. My experiences in psychodrama were nothing short of liberating, and Dorothy and Mort's care and enthusiasm were infectious and healing.

For the insights and personal growth that they made possible, I will be forever grateful. I know I echo the sentiments of hundreds of psychodrama group participants with whom I am personally acquainted, as well as those of many thousands of people I know Dorothy and Mort touched over the years with their healing gifts.

Myself an author, just hours after meeting Dorothy, I recognized the book inside her calling out to be written. It was an honor for me to be her collaborator and scribe in this endeavor, to be a student of psychodrama with her and Mort, and to be a fellow sojourner on this exciting journey of self-discovery and growth. May this book serve to enlighten, entertain, and to inspire all those who read it to take their own journey of self-discovery.

LESLIE CAROL BAER DINKEL
2006/2018

SPECIAL THANKS – *It takes a variety of talents and sensibilities to create a special book such as this. Heartfelt thanks to Dorothy's children, Fred Marshall and Mary Gadzinski, and editor Barbara Smythe, for lending their time and careful copyediting skills to this work; and to designer/editor Betsey Binét for turning the manuscript into an exquisite graphic design worthy of the words of wisdom it showcases.*

Appendix

For X-ray Vision

You can learn to become compassionate with yourself and the people you love by practicing X-ray vision:

1. Get two chairs. Place the chairs facing each other about three feet apart. Choose a chair for yourself, sit down, and close your eyes. Picture someone in your life for whom you've had difficulty feeling compassion. Choose something in the room to represent that person, and place it in the other chair. Make several statements to the object representing that person, and make them from your heart. When you've said all you have to say from that position, move behind your chair, and get little.

2. From behind your chair, go deeper into your heart of hearts where you tell yourself more of the truth, and say what else is true. Make sure and include saying what you could try that would make the relationship better. When it feels right, move back into your own chair.

3. Now, stand up, look around the room for something to represent you, and put it on your chair. Sit in the other chair and "become" the person with whom you have been speaking: Take the body position of that person, become as old or as young as that person. Look across at the object representing you, and respond as that person to what you said to them. Take your time, imagining you have had their life. As you speak, look back at your own chair through their eyes. When you've said all you have to say from that position, move behind their chair.

4. Get little, and from there—deep inside that person's heart of hearts, where they tell themselves more of the truth—speak

what else is also true. Make sure and include what you (as that person) could try that would make the relationship better. When it feels right, move back to the front of their chair.

5. Now, move back to your own chair. From your own chair, speak again. Tell the person what you know you could do to make the relationship better, and why you haven't done it. Move back to the other chair.

6. From there, as the other person, speak about what you know you could do, also, and why you haven't done it. Move back to your own chair.

Take your time with this exercise; relationships are precious. This is called "role-reversal," and the reason to do it is that you cannot create intimacy with any other person except to the extent that you can role-reverse with that person, and look back at yourself through that person's eyes. With your new X-ray vision, you can now look through the other person's chair to the little person speaking from their heart. You can also see more deeply into yourself.

The insights gained from this experience and your newfound X-ray vision will help you to begin building a bridge, instead of a wall. It will help you cultivate compassion for this person and, ultimately, for yourself.

Recommended Reading

For the Lay Audience:

Do I Have to Give Up Me to Be Loved by You?
Jordan Paul, Ph.D., and Margaret Paul, Ph.D. | Hazelden

Teaching Your Children Joy
Richard Eyre, Linda Eyre | Simon & Schuster, New York

Keeping the Love You Find: A Personal Guide
Harville Hendriz, Ph.D. | Pocket Books/Simon & Schuster

Love is Letting Go of Fear
Gerald G. Jampolsky, M.D. | Celestialarts, Berkeley/Toronto

For Mental Health Professionals (and enthusiastic lay people):

Foundations of Psychodrama
Adam Blatner, M.D. | Springer Publishing Company,
New York

The Living Stage
Tian Dayton, Ph.D., T.E.P. | HCI The Life Issues Publisher

Character Styles
Stephen M. Johnson | W.W. Norton, New York/London

Characterological Transformation: The Hard Work Miracle
Stephen M. Johnson | W.W. Norton, New York/London

One Hundred Percent of Profits to Charity

*I*n keeping with Dorothy's mission and passion, upon her death, the family passed this book into the care of her friend and collaborator, Leslie Carol Baer Dinkel, so that the proceeds from *Real is Better Than Perfect* will continue helping others to reach their full potential—the heart and soul of Dorothy's life's work. Through the nonprofit organization Xela AID Partnerships for Self Reliance (aka Local Hope), 100 percent of the profits from this book provide access to health care, education, clean water and other critical resources to those with great need, so that they may live, learn and thrive!

Dorothy Baldwin Satten (right) with Leslita, a young participant in programs sponsored by Xela AID Partnerships for Self Reliance

PUBLISHER AND BENEFICIARY ORGANIZATION

Real is Better Than Perfect has been published in all editions by Hopedancing Publishing, which designates 100 percent of profits from its published books and music to projects that develop human potential. All proceeds from this book benefit the following organization:

Founded in Guatemala in 1992, Xela AID Partnerships for Self Reliance (also known as Local Hope) is a 501(c)(3) nonprofit organization that empowers children and families to break the cycle of poverty and to become healthy, educated and self reliant. To learn more, to sponsor a child to go to school, to become an international volunteer or otherwise become involved, visit xelaaid.org or localhope.org, or contact us at info@xelaaid.org.

Made in the USA
Middletown, DE
12 September 2024